to P.C. – G.A.
for Lucy – N.S.

PANTS
A PICTURE CORGI BOOK 978 0 552 57007 7

First published in Great Britain by David Fickling Books,
a division of Random House Children's Publishers UK

David Fickling edition published 2002
Picture Corgi edition published 2003

Picture Corgi Books are published by Random House Children's Publishers UK,
61–63 Uxbridge Road, London W5 5SA,
A RANDOM HOUSE GROUP COMPANY
Addresses for companies within The Random House
Group Limited can be found
at: www.randomhouse.co.uk/offices.htm

THE RANDOM HOUSE GROUP Limited Reg. No. 954009
www.randomhousechildrens.co.uk

A CIP catalogue record for this book is available from the British Library.

Printed in China

Pants

Giles Andreae
Nick Sharratt

Picture Corgi

Pants

Small pants, big pants

Giant frilly pig pants

New pants, blue pants one, two, three

Loose pants, tight pants

Lighting up at night pants

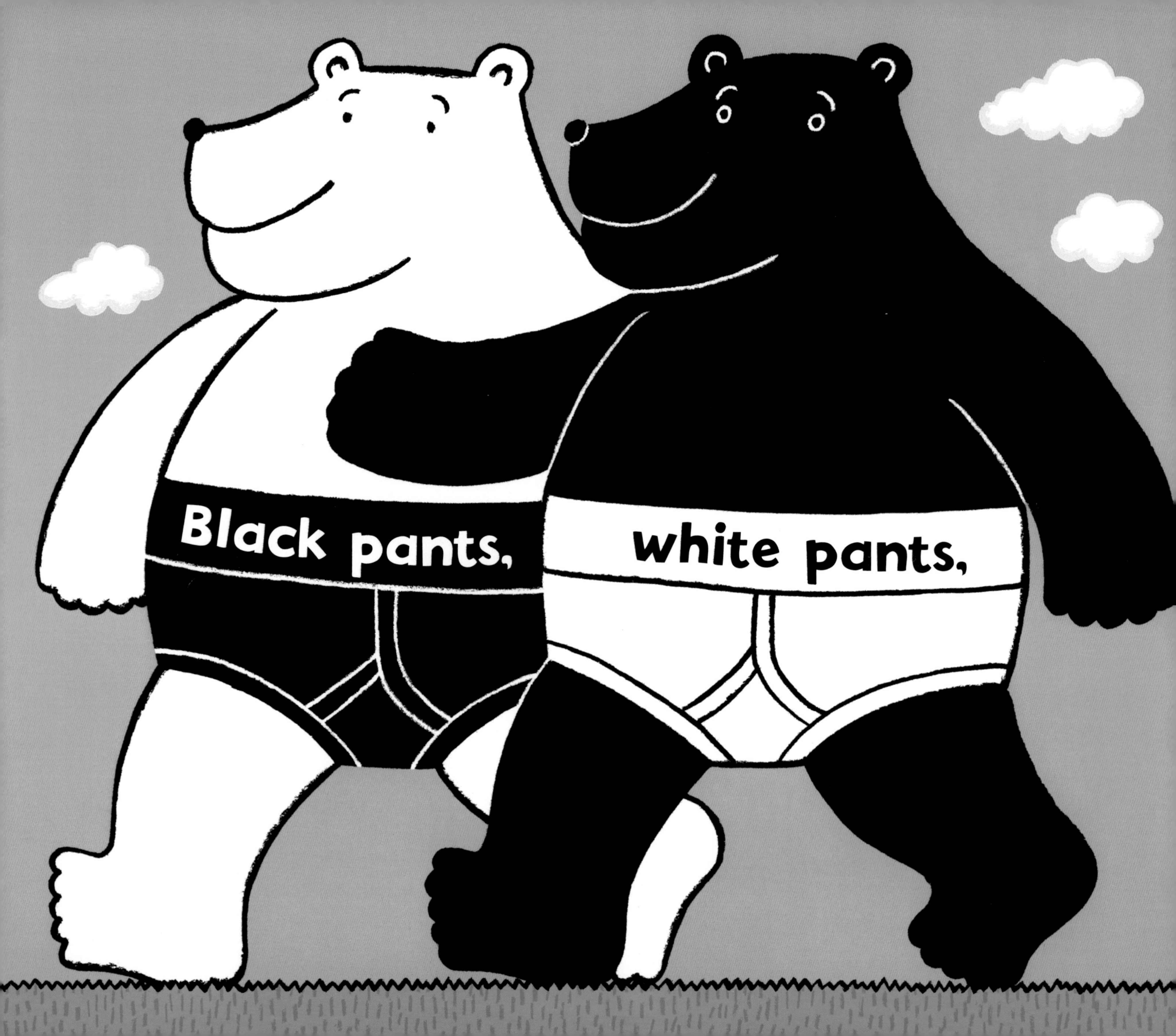
Black pants,
white pants,

no pants at all!

Pants on your head when you've gone crazy!

Funny pants,
money pants

Wear them when it's sunny pants

Have you seen these bunny pants?

– yes I have!

Wear them when
you're happy pants

Fairy pants, hairy pants

What a lot of lovely